ONCE UPON A DREAM

Poets From The East

Edited By Warren Arthur

First published in Great Britain in 2017 by:

Young**Writers**
Est. 1991

Young Writers
Remus House
Coltsfoot Drive
Peterborough
PE2 9BF
Telephone: 01733 890066
Website: www.youngwriters.co.uk

FOREWORD

Welcome to 'Once Upon A Dream – Poets From The East'.

For our 'Once Upon A Dream' competition, we invited primary school pupils to delve within their deepest imaginations and create poetry inspired by dreams. They were not limited to the dreams they experience during their sleep, they were free to explore and describe their dreams and aspirations for the future, what could inspire a dream, and also the darker side of dreams... the nightmare!

The topic proved to be hugely popular, with children dreaming up the cleverest, craziest and, sometimes, creepiest of poems! The entries we received showcase the writing talent and inspired imaginations of today's budding young writers.

Congratulations to Poppy Patnell, who has been selected as the best poet in this anthology, hopefully this is a dream come true! Also a big well done to everyone whose work is included within these pages, I hope seeing it published help you continue living your writing dreams!

Warren Arthur

CONTENTS

Winner:

Poppy Patnell (9) - Sandringham
& West Newton CE Primary   1
School, West Newton

Coldfair Green CP School, Knodishall

Amelia Saunders (8)	3
Harry Nunez (8)	4
Joseph Clements (9)	5
Chester Blake Edmunds (10)	6
Jack Joseph Blizard (9)	7
Heather Samantha Tibbenham (9)	8
Daniel Baldry (9)	9
Harry Mayhew (9)	10

Litcham Primary School, Litcham

Shannon Collison (8)	11
Josiah Weatherill (8)	12
Reece Buxton (8)	14
Noah Bailey (8)	15
Ethan Culligan (8)	16
Angelina Stadames (8)	17
Freya Hussmann (8)	18
Aimee Downes (8)	19
Hayden Sampson (8)	20
Jorjie Reade (8)	21
Tia Mackney (9)	22
Lucas Smith (8)	23
Grace Bruce (7)	24
Louis Peter Westhorpe (8)	25
Freddy Raymond Carmon McLeod (9)	26

Lucas Burrows (8)	27
Tom Watts (9)	28
Harvey Taylor (8)	29
Poppy Annanelle (7)	30
Bradley Winfield (7)	31

Mile Cross Primary School, Norwich

Maria Szimonetta Poczok (9)	32
Ari-Cruz Salih (9)	33
Madison Wicks (9)	34
Adrijana Juzenaite (9)	35
Hayden Jack Sean Stanton (9)	36
Bluebelle Eden Welsh (9)	37
Emilio Jose Betts (8)	38
Kyle Hall (9)	39
Gari Ewing (9)	40
Jayden Bale (9)	41
Leah Reeve (8)	42
Daniel James Newton (9)	43
Oliver Allen (9)	44
Chelsea Thomson (9)	45
Ryan Henry Bristow (9)	46

North Walsham Junior School, North Walsham

Lewis Barker (8)	47
Milly Jones (8)	48

Preston CE (VC) Primary School, Tasburgh

Molly Orford (9)	49
Rosie Scott (9)	50
Millie Laura Jane Skinner (9)	51
Rosie Hesp (9) & Lilly Gall (9)	52
Maisie Eden Tooke (9)	53
Poppy Trayhorn (9)	54
Gracie Elizabeth Scothern (8)	55

Ringshall School, Ringshall

Scott Ali (11)	56
Alex Rodger (10)	58
Chloe Larkin-Smith (10)	60
Romario Haye (10)	62
Rhea Anne Dilworth (10)	63
Rehema Kansonkho (11)	64
Caitlin Kent (10)	65
Jasmine Smith (11)	66
Yetta Likulagi Saumaka (10)	67
Mishka Gurung (9)	68
Tia Leanne Ellis (11)	69
Amelia Gurung (10)	70
Toby Cullum (10)	71

Rushmere Hall Primary School, Ipswich

Harriet Gazeley (10)	72
Zoe Tanner (10)	74
Kate-Anne Platt (10)	75
Evie Mallitt (11)	76
Rebecca Garnett (11)	78
Evie Mackenzie (11)	79
Lola Sargeant (10)	80
Alexander Bark (11)	81
Bryony Seabrook (11)	82
Fraya Garwood (11)	83
Jessica Harvey (11)	84
Emily Hawkridge (10)	85
Olivia Hall (11)	86
Holly Misselbrook (10)	87

Ellen Savage (11)	88
Lilly Grace Matthews (11)	89
Samuel Davey (10)	90
Ashton Symonds (10)	91
Jessica Whiffin (11)	92
Samuel Radley (10)	93
Zander James (11)	94
Lacey Goodwin (10)	95
Lucy Rose Smith (11)	96
Kayleigh Rose Garrett (11)	97

Sandringham & West Newton CE Primary School, West Newton

Gracie Collison (9)	98
Jasper Pike (9)	100
Nina Daisy Fowler (9)	101
Tyler Kerry (9)	102
Jack James Miller (9)	103
Henry Benjamin James (9)	104
Maddy Taylor (9)	105
Lilly Clare Hickling (8)	106
Clara Elizabeth Moreland (8)	107
Jasmina Gadiwala (9)	108
Sienna May (8)	109
Thomas Strudwick (8)	110
Chloe Southwell (8)	111
Ella Southwell (8)	112
Giovanni Giubileo (8)	113
Taylor Ashton Winsor (9)	114
Stanley Thomas Farr-James (8)	115
Kateryna Musgrave (8)	116

St Felix RC Primary School, Haverhill

Franciszek Teliczan (10)	117
Eluned Morgan-Owen (9) & Grace	118
Kathy Ann Wirowski (10)	119
Jasmine Nungari Marshall (10)	120
Nakita Van Aswegen (10)	121
Claudia Bergin (9)	122
Cody Armstrong (9)	123

Tyler Cardoso (9)	124
Oscar Clay (9)	125
Anna-Grace Mathew (10)	126
Ryan Hammond (9)	127
Juvi Danielle Sason Carandang (9)	128
Hollie Buckingham (10)	129
Sofia Emily Rinaldi (9)	130
Lucy Murrell (10)	131
Zoe Olivia Boreham (9)	132
Joshua King (9)	133
Marta Grzegorczyk (9)	134
Evie Grace Naylor (8)	135
Cahir Catherine Williams (9)	136
Catherine Anne Theresa Goring (9)	137
Luca Lambert (9)	138
Weronika Lubinska (9)	139
Felix Jose (9)	140
Michal Wargin (10)	141
Maya Glowacki (9)	142
Alexandra Graham (8)	143

Swanton Abbott Community Primary School, Swanton Abbott

Emily Rose Morton (8)	144
Ellie Simmons (9)	145
Millie Isabel Karim (9)	146
Isabella McKnespiey (9)	147
Rebecca Mae Strawson (8)	148
Louise Hurrell (9)	149
Cia Smith (9)	150
Halle Mynett-Smith (8)	151
Oliver Bunton-Butler (8)	152
Mia Lofty (8)	153
Lyra Hall (8)	154
Ellie Summer Oakley (9)	155
Freddie Wilson (8)	156
Thomas Aldous (7)	157
Max Brackpool (8)	158

THE POEMS

The Adventure

The pencil stared and rubbed its eyes.
All around him were sobs and cries.
A sharpener, ruler and a green felt tip.
All struggling, failing to undo the zip.
Like a hero, I clasp it, pull it back
Careful at first, just a crack
I take a peep out of the hole
Feeling like a springtime mole.
Children leaving for the night
A tired teacher turns out the light.
I pull out the stationery one by one,
'Come on,' I shout, 'let's have some fun.'
But too much excitement's not good for my health.
I'm dizzy, I trip, fall behind the shelf
But then a pale hand reaches round
Hooray! I have been found!
I'm popped into a pocket with a lovely smell
She's an artist, I can tell.

I wake to find
I dreamt it all,
So I grab my pencil and I'm off to school!

Poppy Patnell (9)
Sandringham & West Newton CE Primary School, West Newton

Competition Time

They heard a bell ringing in the big room,
It was time for Holly, Me, Lexi and Chloe to do our
competition.
They did their floor work all together.
When they were in the middle, they heard a thump and
a jump,
Boom! The door opened.
It was an evil witch, she grabbed Chloe's horse.
They all stopped and went outside, they were trying to
catch her.
Suddenly, they heard a bang, a huff and a puff, it was
Phoebe.
The witch ran off.
Phoebe was hurt, they went to the vets and she was
fine.
She just had a bad stomach, they said she had to rest.
They all went back to the competition
And they got a 10:0 like a shimmering glimmering star.

Amelia Saunders (8)
Coldfair Green CP School, Knodishall

The Island

It was as hot as the sun when we were on the boat.
We were going to an island that had been lost forever.
It had a volcano as black as coal, palm trees taller than an oak tree.
But nothing had prepared us for what they were going to see next.
As they walked through the lush forest,
Jason the dog barked.
So we followed him, he led us to a nest.
There were two eggs that hatched into a dragon and a dinosaur.
In horror we ran.
But a dragon dive-bombed my friends.
I was with Jason, we wanted to save them,
So we climbed up a steep mountain
And then we were on the top. I woke up!

Harry Nunez (8)
Coldfair Green CP School, Knodishall

The Kitchen Land!

I walked into the kitchen.
I couldn't believe the sight that my eyes were seeing.
My mind drifted away like a kite.
I saw dancing cups and plates and talking
silver toasters.
Ten out of ten, ten out of ten, they're my mates.
There were running chopping boards
With silver butter knives.
I saw talking potted trees.
I wish I hadn't arrived.
I saw a pirate in a cruise ship,
He came and made me happy,
As happy as a bunny.
Bang! I woke up.
Why did I find that funny?

Joseph Clements (9)
Coldfair Green CP School, Knodishall

The Clown Chase

I visit a football stadium called Tottenham
With a few of my friends and played some football.
Then suddenly, a clown in an ambulance
As big as a helicopter pushed through a barrier.
He had a chainsaw...
We weaved in and out of the football stadium.
He threw a potion at us.
We heard the sirens
We ow, we ow, we no!
It was the police,
We were safe.
I woke up
Phew!
It was just a dream.

Chester Blake Edmunds (10)
Coldfair Green CP School, Knodishall

The Sweet Dream

I was in this weird Sweet Land.
With my two friends Daniel and Jake.
The sweets looked like wheat.
The beetroot was called Wheatroot
The house were made out of candy.
But instead of people working,
there were robots.
Unicorns ate sweets called gummy props
So we had a try of these sweets.
They were hotter than lava.
The sun was a sweet.
It was sour, well the sourest
Warhead ever made.

Jack Joseph Blizard (9)
Coldfair Green CP School, Knodishall

The Magical Land

I visited a magical world with Lily.
There were fairies and unicorns.
We felt excited and nervous.
There was a shell that kept the colours of the rainbow.
One morning the shell was gone.
Lily and Heather looked everywhere.
Then we looked in the water.
There it was, the shell has been found.
We took the shell out.
Then all the colours were back together.
It was magical!

Heather Samantha Tibbenham (9)
Coldfair Green CP School, Knodishall

The Goal

In front of 100,000,000 people.
I've just received the ball.
Their defence is like a brick wall.
I smash the ball past the defender
They would start to surrender.
I run past them.
Like a group of hens.
Then run into the box.
Past Mr Fox.
Smash! Bang! I score!
It feels like a dream.
I hear the country singing as loud as a bomb.

Daniel Baldry (9)
Coldfair Green CP School, Knodishall

Living Island

I had a dream about a tree that spoke of all he'd seen,
from the Romans to the Victorians.
Bob the plant and I talked and listened,
I was feeling happy then a flying meerkat came out of
a bush.
There was dancing bananas near a tree.
All I had to eat was the dancing bananas!
All I had to do was listen to the tree,
Then I woke up and it was just a dream.

Harry Mayhew (9)
Coldfair Green CP School, Knodishall

Northern Lights

Waving, shining, sparkling,
Northern Lights, Northern Lights
Just like a rainbow
Northern Lights, Northern Lights
Swishing, swaying, lighting the sky
Northern Lights, Northern Lights
Shining as bright as the sun
Northern Lights, Northern Lights
Just like the Grinch fading away in the distance
Northern Lights, Northern Lights
Twirling, glowing, shining,
Northern Lights, Northern Lights
As colourful as a kaleidoscope
Northern Lights, Northern Lights
Lighting the sky just like diamonds
Northern Lights, Northern Lights.

Shannon Collison (8)
Litcham Primary School, Litcham

A Day In The Ocean

Deep down in the ocean
Searching for treasure I saw
Eight electrifying eels.

In the ocean of dreams
I saw a leafy sea dragon
Drifting the seven seas
A sea dragon like a leaf
Under the sea, under the sea.

In the ocean of depths
I saw a bowhead whale
Swimming in the ocean
A bowhead whale as big as a bus
Under the sea, under the sea

In the ocean of dreams
I saw a dolphin
Leaping the huge waves
Skin as silky as a scarf
Under the sea, under the sea

In the ocean of depths
I saw a jellyfish
Drifting the depths

A fish is a jelly
Under the sea, under the sea

In the ocean of dreams
I saw a pufferfish
Puffing up.
A puffer is blown up like a ball
Under the sea, under the sea.

In the ocean of depths
I saw a shark
Surfing the sea floor
A shark's tooth as sharp as a knife
Under the sea, under the sea.

In the ocean of dreams
I saw a seahorse
Drifting the ocean
A fish is a horse
Under the sea, under the sea.

Josiah Weatherill (8)
Litcham Primary School, Litcham

Sealife You Can See

In the deep, deep sea this is what you'll see
Five jellyfish dancing in the sea
That's what you'll see...

In the deep, deep sea this is what you'll eat
Green, green seaweed slimy but tasty
That's what you'll eat...

In the deep, deep sea this is what you'll feel
Soft, soft sand in the wild waves
That's what you'll feel...

In the deep, deep sea this is what you'll touch
Beautiful seashells smooth and shiny
That's what you'll touch...

Reece Buxton (8)
Litcham Primary School, Litcham

Falling Off A Surfing Board

When I fell off a surfing board
I saw a pufferfish coming towards me.
When I fell off a surfing board I touched sea grass.
When I fell off a surfing board I heard a whale calling
When I fell off a surfing board I tasted the salt.
When I fell off a surfing board I smelt fish food.
The rocks were as big as mountains.
The grass tickled like feathers.
The shark was a devil
The angelfish was an angel.
There was a tank which went *bang!*
There was an under the sea choir.

Noah Bailey (8)
Litcham Primary School, Litcham

A Day In The Ocean

In the ocean I got...
Chased by a shark
The scary one.

In the ocean I got...
Bitten by a water snake
The painful one.

In the ocean I got...
Scared by an eel
The protective one

In the ocean I got
Inked by a squid
As inky as a pen.

In the ocean I got...
Shocked by a fish
While it was dancing.

In the ocean I got...
Chomped by a lion-fish
The pig!

What a day!

Ethan Culligan (8)
Litcham Primary School, Litcham

Haiku Poetry

Spring
Baby chicks are born
The trees' leaves are growing fast
Baby lambs are born.

Summer
The sun is shining
T-shirts and pink shorts put on
Birds sing in the sun.

Autumn
Chocolate ice cream
Getting ready for harvest
Going to the beach.

Winter
Cold ice on the road
It is fun making snowmen
Drink hot chocolate.

Angelina Stadames (8)
Litcham Primary School, Litcham

Northern Lights

Twirling, glowing, shining
Northern Lights, Northern Lights
Shapes like a ghost
Northern Lights, Northern Lights
Green swirling smoke in the sky
Northern Lights, Northern Lights
Red, green, purple, blue, any colour at all
Northern Lights, Northern Lights
Glittery, long, bright, beautiful
Northern Lights, Northern Lights
Sparkling like the sky
Northern Lights, Northern Lights.

Freya Hussmann (8)
Litcham Primary School, Litcham

In The Ocean Of My Dreams

Down in the ocean I saw a dolphin.
Down in the dark sea I saw a shark.

Ten seahorses dancing through the deep sea.
Nine fish swimming through the sea.

In the ocean of my dreams

Seven jellyfish jumping on jelly
Six octopuses swimming
While dancing through the deep sea
Five angelfish singing through the sea.

Aimee Downes (8)
Litcham Primary School, Litcham

Deep-Sea Diver

The sharks were eating eels
All the sharks were protecting their little ones.
Five sneaky sharks sitting on the seabed.

Jellyfish fighting over jelly
Jellyfish purple, pink and blue
Jellyfish bouncing on jelly.

I saw a squid squirting ink,
I should have brought a pen.
I felt a squid tickle me under the chin.

Hayden Sampson (8)
Litcham Primary School, Litcham

In The Ocean

In the ocean of dreams I saw...
Two dancing dolphins swimming in the water.

In the ocean of dreams I saw...
Ten fun seahorses playing in the seaweed.

In the ocean of dreams I saw...
Four scared catfish hiding in the seaweed.

In the ocean of dreams I saw...
Eleven pufferfish puffing to the surf water.

Jorjie Reade (8)
Litcham Primary School, Litcham

Under The Water

Down deep, deep in the deep blue sea, here was I.
I swam through the sea
which was shimmering like a whale.
The seaweed waved at me.
I was captured by a seahorse
when I saw it come swaying over to me.
It put me in a cave,
when it was gone a mermaid rescued me.
I swam across the ocean
when I saw some mermaids glaring at me.

Tia Mackney (9)
Litcham Primary School, Litcham

Deep-Sea Diving

In the deep, deep sea
I saw five frightening fish
Calming down after a fight.

In the deep, deep sea
I saw two octopuses
Having a marriage.

In the deep, deep sea
I saw one lovely cute dolphin
Looking for a friend.

In the deep, deep sea
I saw one friendly shark
Giving me a hug.

Lucas Smith (8)
Litcham Primary School, Litcham

Helping Undersea Animals

Down at the deep, deep sea
I could see dancing dolphins.
Down in the deep, dark sea
I saw goldfish swimming really fast.
Down in the dark sea
I saw goldfish swimming really fast.
Down helping injured fish,
I saw a scary shark.
Down in the deep sea helping pufferfish
I saw thirty goldfish swimming really fast!

Grace Bruce (7)
Litcham Primary School, Litcham

Haiku Poems

Blossom trees falling
Baby chicks are born in trees
Lots of birds singing.

Chocolate ice cream
Getting ready for harvest
Going to the beach.

Going back to school
Leaves are falling off the trees
Halloween party!

Santa coming soon
The Grinch is fading away
Nativity plays.

Louis Peter Westhorpe (8)
Litcham Primary School, Litcham

Deep Below The Sea

In the sea I saw five bull sharks pretending they're one.
In the sea I saw one seahorse.
In the sea I saw one fast pupfish.
In the sea I saw a swimming fish.
In the sea I saw a jellyfish fighting over jelly.
In the sea I saw a shark biting my nose.
In the sea I saw a naughty crab biting my toes.

Freddy Raymond Carmon McLeod (9)

Litcham Primary School, Litcham

Epic Riddles!

I am big and hairy
I've got a head and two eyes, no tail
What am I?

I am see-through
I can open
I have not got a head
What am I?

I'm shiny and black,
I can be blue, white, red, grey and yellow
I've got an engine
What am I?

Lucas Burrows (8)
Litcham Primary School, Litcham

In The Ocean

Jellyfish biting
Jellyfish stinging.

Jellyfish stinging viciously
Jellyfish being hungry.

Jellyfish as powerful as a power line
Jellyfish as fast as lightning.

Jellyfish jumping in the sea
Jellyfish diving swimming sponges.

Tom Watts (9)
Litcham Primary School, Litcham

Haiku Poetry

Springtime birds singing
Leaves all falling on the floor
Baby chicks are born.

People at the beach
Eating lots of ice cream
The sun in the sky.

Going back to school
Seeing my amazing friends
Playing games is fun.

Harvey Taylor (8)
Litcham Primary School, Litcham

Haiku Poems

Blossom trees swaying
Lots of animals are born
Mountains are freezing.

Chocolate ice cream
Getting ready for harvest
Going to the beach.

Going back to school
Leaves are falling off the trees
Halloween party.

Poppy Annanelle (7)
Litcham Primary School, Litcham

Ocean Of Dreams

In the ocean of dreams I saw
One hundred sharks swimming in the Atlantic Ocean.

In the ocean of dreams I saw
Seven starfish dancing in the sea.

In the ocean of dreams I saw
A jellyfish dancing.

Bradley Winfield (7)
Litcham Primary School, Litcham

Once Upon A Dream

I got lost, what can I do?
I'm a lovely girl too.
Where should I go, I forget the way?
Which is the way?
I love dancing
Singing and acting.
Hope I just need two minutes to realise which is the way.
But anyway I head somewhere safe
Then I realise where is the way
But then it's too late
Because I realise a woman is following me.
Oh, then I just wake up and say, 'Oh yay, it is just a dream.'

Maria Szimonetta Poczok (9)
Mile Cross Primary School, Norwich

Canopic Jar

C urling and twirling around
A s Jayden and I discover the world
N ot a nice smell
O range clay on the jars from underground
P icture in your head, the jars
I wonder and wonder if I'll find a tomb?
C reatures creeping around

J ayden is bashing the walls down and digging
A lways searching
R unning in excitement as we find a tomb...

Ari-Cruz Salih (9)
Mile Cross Primary School, Norwich

Once Upon A Dream!

One lovely morning, the sun was shining bright,
Although I was not always Mr Right,
What a lovely day, I saw a unicorn
Although your little horns smelled a bit like corn
The sparkle in your eyes glowing in the night
Although you did give me a little fright
So I woke up one morning and said, 'Oh it was a dream
I may call that my once upon a dream!'

Madison Wicks (9)
Mile Cross Primary School, Norwich

My Worst Nightmare

It's dark and scary
Every minute I get frightened
I see a clown as I run away
The clown chases me anyway
As I run further, the clown gets lost
But I get lost too
As I get more frightened it gets darker
I've been out all night
But wait I see a light
I run as fast as I can
But I am wrong it's not a light
It is a monster!

Adrijana Juzenaite (9)
Mile Cross Primary School, Norwich

Breaking Down

I'm boarding a plane in a crowd
Lifting into the air next to my co-pilot who doesn't
know I'm there.
Feeling nervous as smoke comes out of my left engine
My plane is near Las Vegas
People screaming as power cuts out!
Plane hits Las Vegas,
Waking up as rubble is on my head
Plane lights up with fire
Plane explodes with my life.

Hayden Jack Sean Stanton (9)
Mile Cross Primary School, Norwich

Once Upon A Dream

Dreams are like stars
They come and go
but the ones that stay
are the ones that glow.
Repeat and disappear
They go in a fairy-tale blare
It's like a switch, it goes on and off
Some dreams even make you cough
Other dreams make you smile
In some dreams you run a mile.

Bluebelle Eden Welsh (9)
Mile Cross Primary School, Norwich

Good Dreams, Bad Dreams, Perfect Dreams

The Greek books bloody, beheaded like Medusa
If you want more blood and guts, look at
Shakespeare's bad luck.
Don't forget the story of the tortoise and hare.
A story of torture and despair.
These are the dreams I want to make,
Just when I am awake.

Emilio Jose Betts (8)
Mile Cross Primary School, Norwich

Funny Dream

Mummy dummy
Ollie in the holly
Nighty tighty
Kyle pile.

Electric hectic
Yummy, gummy
Football is the test
Tennis is the best

Money honey
Death bead
Hair tear
Bed head
But it was all a funny dream.

Kyle Hall (9)
Mile Cross Primary School, Norwich

My Dream To Be In A Knight World

I am a wizard making magic
Magic sparkling all around
Sparkles tilting around
Magic light lighting
I am a nice wizard
Marking magic
Flashing everywhere
Bright bangs like fireworks
And my dream is to be a wizard.

Gari Ewing (9)
Mile Cross Primary School, Norwich

Dreams

D reams can always come true

R hythm of your dream is always good

E verybody's dreams will always say be yourself

A ri carries a football in my dreams

M ake it funny

S o live your life.

Jayden Bale (9)
Mile Cross Primary School, Norwich

School

S ymmetry flowing

C ool dudes growing

H ouses melting made from snow and ice

O range bands pulling

O rangutans jumping

L ooking like mice, to spy the rice.

Leah Reeve (8)
Mile Cross Primary School, Norwich

Super Daniel

My name is Daniel
And I am eight
I never look a disgrace
I dream of flying
And I do good deeds
In my dream.
I am... Super Daniel!

Daniel James Newton (9)
Mile Cross Primary School, Norwich

The Football Players

Football is the best
Players do not rest
When the ball comes to them
They smash it if they can
Arsenal are the best!

Oliver Allen (9)
Mile Cross Primary School, Norwich

Cats

C ats are the best
A nd they are fluffy
T eachers are good at teaching
S pecial as a diamond.

Chelsea Thomson (9)
Mile Cross Primary School, Norwich

Chocolate Land

I can see a big red foot
And another foot in a chocolate waterfall
With some strawberries.
They are big.

Ryan Henry Bristow (9)
Mile Cross Primary School, Norwich

Bee Nonsense!

You have a rather large ear,
Can you hear the red deer?
The red deer stole my gear in my car.

An alien called Zar,
Has run off with my car
When I got distracted by a bee.
Who flew to a flea
And it fell to one knee
I ran to a tree.

Lewis Barker (8)
North Walsham Junior School, North Walsham

Untitled

I woke up,
The morning sun was shining in my eyes.
Goodbye famous fairies,
Flying dancers, royalty, pirates,
Getting lost monsters, dragons,
Famous writers, wizards, unicorns,
Dinosaurs and dragons.

Milly Jones (8)
North Walsham Junior School, North Walsham

Wings

I pull the covers up over my face and close my
weary eyes,
When I open them again I am standing,
Standing on my window sill and opening the window
I jump off, out into the open air,
Confused, I don't fall down to my peril,
But glide swiftly along,
I find a pair of wings have sprouted straight from
my back,
They are dazzling multicoloured wings,
Maybe of a screeching tropical bird,
It is only then do I realise that I am really flying,
Flying on a gentle summer breeze that warms me,
I feel a sense of freedom and pure joy,
I spread my wings, the wind in my hair
Then I begin falling, falling, falling and, *thump!*
I wake up and wish it had been real

Molly Orford (9)
Preston CE (VC) Primary School, Tasburgh

The Whirl Of A Wave

I was paddling happily in the sea,
When something suddenly grabbed at me,
It was a whirling tidal wave,
That pulled me into a tunnelling cave,
It spun me round like a washing machine
And pushed me to a bright shining beam,
It was really scary, but then I saw,
Hundreds of seahorses on the sea floor.
They tugged me upwards, gasping for air.
Other sorts of seahorses were racing there,
They led me to an island with a dazzling lake,
And suddenly I found that I was wide awake!

Rosie Scott (9)
Preston CE (VC) Primary School, Tasburgh

Rosie Fairy!

My name is Rosie,
I have a friend called Posy
And we are fairies!
Today we're going to see if the pink waterfall is okay.
Now we're having fun in the sun!
Now we are seeing Isabelle.
At the minute she's in hell!
The other day my friend left
But... it was pretend!
Now it's time for bed,
But we wanted to play instead.
My best friend is Lily,
She can be a little bit silly!
Now we wake
And then take a break.

Millie Laura Jane Skinner (9)
Preston CE (VC) Primary School, Tasburgh

Cookies

Some are big, some are small,
Some even come from the mall.
They're all shapes and sizes,
Some have chocolate chips,
Some have sultanas
And some have weird bits

They're nice with sprinkles
They're nice with icing
They're nice with marshmallows
But not when they are mouldy.

Hope you enjoyed our cookie poem,
And we hope it made you raid the cupboards for...
Cookies!

Rosie Hesp (9) & Lilly Gall (9)
Preston CE (VC) Primary School, Tasburgh

The Magic Land!

Thousands of stars surround me as I get whisked to
another land!
Hundreds of thoughts come into my head
I don't know
what to do!
Enormous castles, buildings and houses, where can I
be?
Maybe I'm dreaming, maybe I'm not!
Am I here or am I not?
Ahead I see, I see a library.
Why do I see a library?
I see a library, I see a library!

Maisie Eden Tooke (9)
Preston CE (VC) Primary School, Tasburgh

Bedtime

I pull the covers above my head
And tuck myself up into bed.
I dream my dream and hum my song
Let's hope I don't smell a pong!
I shut my eyes and fall asleep
I don't find it helpful counting sheep.
In the morning I wake up, I rub my eyes and I see
A pair of eyes staring at me.

Poppy Trayhorn (9)
Preston CE (VC) Primary School, Tasburgh

Dancing And Prancing

D aring boys and girls prancing around
A mazing flips and tricks
N oisy children, fun and laughter
C areful spins through the air
I enjoy dancing everywhere
N ow come and join in
G et to make lots of friends, while getting in a spin.

Gracie Elizabeth Scothern (8)
Preston CE (VC) Primary School, Tasburgh

Dream Quest

Four sullen walls,
Casting a shadow over the village
Villagers dare not step in
This haunted building.

A tall oak door
Planted in the wall
Beyond this door
Awaits the great reward.

A journey through,
This haunted place
If you survive,
You will receive a great reward.

Creak! the floor
Creaks under your weight.
This old building
Sustains the prize.

Drip, drop, drip,
You hear running water,
This noise you head towards,
Is this a trap?

Back at the door,
Crestfallen with the result
But luckily alive.

Will the village,
Ever know
What the prize maybe?

Scott Ali (11)
Ringshall School, Ringshall

A New World To Kiss

Clouds carry me far away;
They take me to a magical land
Where animals fly;
Chattering to each other.
Where birds have arms instead of wings.

Plants grow quickly
Like they have a spring underneath them;
They sing merry songs
There is no rain to be seen;
Because the clouds are happy.

The sun is wearing sunglasses;
at nightfall the sun has a nap.
The moon dances a tango with the stars,
before sunlight;
Until the sun wakes.

The waterhole is so large and wide
But still it doesn't evaporate
Animals all eat ice cream,
Then fly for evermore;
In the sky.

The leaves on the trees are green and beautiful;
There are no leaves to be seen on the ground

Colourful butterflies swiftly flutter past me,
As my heart leaps and jumps for joy;
Hoping for more.

Suddenly, the clouds come back to me,
They take me away from the magical land
They bring me back home,
They take me up to bed,
As Mum comes up calling and shouting...

Wake up Arnold, you'll be late for school!

I slowly open my eyes and raise my head,
Wishing so much I could sneak back into my dream.
But suddenly, I see a butterfly on my bedside,
Which makes me wonder if my dream has happened
Has it?

Alex Rodger (10)
Ringshall School, Ringshall

The Dragon Show

The bright sun shining over the village
A golden house lay on a grassland
with candy laid around.

The beautiful animals gather
A waterhole with rocks
The rainbow shines
Dragons arrive.

They race through the sky
Creating a show
Breathing fire to make a symbol
Dragons can be seen from anywhere
So fast, good-looking.

Drip, drip, drip, raindrops come down
It starts raining
The animals and people gather
Dragons land on the ground
Thump!
The ground shakes

Night-time comes
The dragons sleep
Under the night sky.

Dragons twisting and turning
Sleeping on the nice green ground
Some in trees
The dragons awake

The bright sun shining over the village
A golden house lay on a grassland
With candy laid around.

Chloe Larkin-Smith (10)
Ringshall School, Ringshall

Dreamland

What a beautiful Dreamland
The birds are singing
The sun smiles which spreads the light around
The lake shimmers like stars
The grass sways left to right.
The animals stand there majestically
Then out of nowhere the land slips
With an emerald glow in the sky
The birds fly beneath my feet
The sun smiles next to me
Majestic animals are above my head
Grass sways over me
The land slips over again
Then I wake up!
What a calm amazing dream
I need some milk to fall asleep
OK I have my milk
I'm back in my Dreamland!
The grass is still swaying left to right
The lake is here, everything is as I remember
Flash!
I wake up again saying what an amazing dream!

Romario Haye (10)
Ringshall School, Ringshall

Superpowers

Suddenly, I could fly
Up, up near the sun
Peeking through the clouds
Every day I would go high
Rain began to fall
People kept asking me where I'd been
Oh, how wonderful it would be.
With all my might I began to fly
Even higher than any other day
Racing ahead I began to dive
Soaring through the bright blue sky.

Rhea Anne Dilworth (10)
Ringshall School, Ringshall

My Paris Dream

Last night I had a dream about Paris...
As I walked through the city of love I heard,
The sweet sound of the violin
As it spread its beautiful music.
I smelt the crispy croissants cooking in the oven.
I saw the gates of Disneyland smile
As they welcomed happy children.
I tasted the cold as ice smoothie
As it ran down my throat,
Sending a tingling sensation of happiness through
my body.
I felt the power of love as it possessed people
around me.

Rehema Kansonkho (11)
Ringshall School, Ringshall

Untitled

Wizard, wizard out in space.
Ready to bake a nice cake.
Here and there searching the sky,
'Mmm,' went the wizard, 'that smells nice.'
He opened the oven and *kaboom!* went the cake.

Here we go again a little bit of flour
A little bit of eggs, a little bit of butter too.
Then a bit of sugar and a little bit of milk.
Mix it all together and put it in the oven
Kaboom! went the cake again.

Caitlin Kent (10)
Ringshall School, Ringshall

Magical Unicorn Friends

The unicorns flew over the rainbow,
The others followed
Way up in the fluffy clouds again.

The sky was warm and birds were singing,
Everything was normal,
The trees were swaying from side to side,
Whilst the sun was shining brightly in the wild sky.

The ocean blue, sparkly winged unicorn
Flew over the brightly coloured rainbow.
The rainbow was floating above the clouds
As the unicorns flew over it for the very last time.

Jasmine Smith (11)
Ringshall School, Ringshall

Candy Land

When I wake up I am in Candy Land,
I pinch my hand to see,
If I will wake.
Then I see a giant chocolate cake!
I smell a wee scent of caramel.
I find a house just for me,
With a garden full of sweets.
The chimney is a muffin,
The roof is melted chocolate.
The plants around my house are cotton candy.
Walk into my house,
You will smell bubblegum
And strawberry.
I really love my crispy yummy house
I eat sometimes in the heat.

Yetta Likulagi Saumaka (10)
Ringshall School, Ringshall

Unisaur

I am a unisaur
A unicorn crossed with a dinosaur.
I have a long pink horn
And a purple fluffy tail
I roar like a lion
And jump like a kangaroo
But what I can't do is
Juggle on one foot
I am a unisaur
I live on a small island
Where all lazy unisaurs go
And I'm the most happiest one of them all
I'm a unisaur
As weird as can be
I'm off to Disneyland,
Please don't stare at me!

Mishka Gurung (9)
Ringshall School, Ringshall

Dreaming Dragons

I woke up,
Looked out my window,
Saw a dragon
Staring,
I stared back,
Flapped his wings at me,
I flew,
Like a bird in the sky
I flew way up high,
Closed my eyes and opened them again,
I was no longer in the sky,
I was somewhere different
I felt scared and different
Where's Mum? Where's Dad?
So I closed my eyes and opened them,
I was home with Mum and Dad again!

Tia Leanne Ellis (11)
Ringshall School, Ringshall

I Have Got Everything

I strolled through my Jade Palace,
With security guards by my side,
I walked through the tall doors
Which were like a giraffe
I have got everything I want.

For breakfast, I had cotton candy clouds.
I savoured the luxurious taste,
Filling my mind.
I have got everything I want!

Amelia Gurung (10)
Ringshall School, Ringshall

Under The Sea

Vroom, vroom;
A bus;
Waiting for me;
Ready to take me under the sea;
Ready to show me the fish and seaweed;
Ready to show me the sharp-toothed sharks;
Ready to show me the ocean's children;
Shimmering sea wait for me!

Toby Cullum (10)
Ringshall School, Ringshall

Glitter Ville

I dreamed of a place, a place that no one knows,
A place with lots of unicorns, a place with a
broken hose,
A place with flying fairies, a place where houses are
pink toadstools,
A place with lots of glitter and sweeties,
I dreamed of a place, a place that no one knows,
A place where I could smell candyfloss that I sniffed up
through my nose,
I dreamed of a place, a place that no one knows,
A place called Glitter Ville, a place that's made of
magic, a place where no one's ill.
I dreamed of a place, a place that no one knows.
A place where my puppy started flying
A place where I got superpowers,
A place where everyone is flying,
I dreamed of a place, a place that no one knows,
A place where no one dies, a place where no one lies
A place that is fun forever, a place where there is
always good weather,
I dreamed of a place, a place that no one knows,
A place called Glitter Ville, a place where I no longer
exist,

A place that is now a distant memory,
A place where my time is gone,
I have woken up.

Harriet Gazeley (10)
Rushmere Hall Primary School, Ipswich

My Dream

Here's the story of my dream,
It started nice, then turned mean.

Gems sparkled oh so bright,
Piercing the darkness of the night
Although there's so much beauty in this cave,
There is something missing, something I crave.

The walls began moving, closing in on me
The beauty was taunting, the last thing I'd see,
How could something so perfect, become so wrong?
I tried to push back, but the force was too strong.

The air was running out: I struggled to breathe
The anger inside me, began to seethe
I couldn't die like this, I needed to get out.
I did the only thing possible - began to shout.
I opened my mouth but out came no noise
I then lost my remaining grace and poise
I thought of my future, I thought of my past
Screaming, I woke up, in my bed at last.

Zoe Tanner (10)
Rushmere Hall Primary School, Ipswich

My Own Little Land

I had a dream one day, about a secret land,
A place that no one knows about,
A place with no clouds, I wonder if you've ever been there?
The sky is always blue, I wish I could be there with you.
A nice place to go like Paris, London, Tokyo,
Except made up in my mind,
Where lots of mythical creatures have lives,
The waterfalls are crystal too,
The trees like cotton candy,
Everything is fine and dandy, in my beautiful secret land.
The unicorns have rainbow tails, the trolls locked up in dungeons,
Smells of the river send a meaningful shiver, that goes down my spine,
A wave of happiness floods the land, like the floods in Somerset.
But just as I begin the adventure,
I wake up at last, my little head full of thoughts, all fit to burst.

Kate-Anne Platt (10)
Rushmere Hall Primary School, Ipswich

Not Me

People dream,
Not me.

People dream of objectives
Not me.

I dream of the future,
I dream of a profession,
When I drive criminals to their confession.
I dream of a bump,
Over that bump
Is Donald Trump.
That bump is a wall,
Over which Trump should fall,
Into jail they'll make him crawl.
He'll be so angry he'll go red in the face
Up and down that cell he will pace
Until he has to race
To do up his shoelace.
The truth he will have to face
That is the case.
All those holes he did dig
Should turn him into a pig.
Just as the dream was ending
Then I had something to dread

Donald Trump was back.
Oh no, I'd better pack.
He gave me a right old smack,
'You're dead,' he said
Then I woke up in bed.

Evie Mallitt (11)
Rushmere Hall Primary School, Ipswich

Once Upon A Nightmare

The streets were bare,
As she walked through them without a care,
If she only knew that the terror was real,
Then she would of been back for a family meal.
Her mum and dad were expecting her back by seven,
But the only place she was going was heaven,
The scarlet monster dripping down her top,
She was too young for the chop,
Her family and friends are filled with sadness,
As the killer is filled with madness,
As he sits in jail,
Every day seems so pale,
Her friend's minds have gone dark,
But to think this all happened at the local park,
Not everyone liked her,
Because of all the trouble she liked to stir,
But this didn't have to happen to her.

Rebecca Garnett (11)
Rushmere Hall Primary School, Ipswich

Nightmare Terror

Shocked and forgotten,
I feel unloved. Do they really care for me?
My mind's a fog of thoughts.
A flicker of hope has gone.
Sadness dripping down my cold face,
No words coming out of my dry mouth.
Stomach is big, twisted in knots.
Shut in a room with so many doors
Don't know what one to pick.
I feel like my parents have badly betrayed me.
Two more days until terror torture.
Heart thumping like a drum, sweat dripping beneath
my thumb.
Tears run down my face, butterflies fly in my tum.
I'm sharply stabbed in my boneless back.
Forgotten what trust is, my father was my only hope.
I'm stuck with no hope and the truth is the truth.

Evie Mackenzie (11)
Rushmere Hall Primary School, Ipswich

I'm A Wizard

I'm a wizard,
A fireball shooting wizard.
Bringing down a dragon,
Then some archers.

I'm a wizard,
A fireball shooting wizard
Killing the enemies,
Saving the village.

I'm a wizard,
A fireball shooting wizard.
Destroy the walls and gold mines,
Destroy all the defences and defenders too.

I'm a wizard,
A fireball shooting wizard
Taking all the available loot.

I'm a wizard,
A fireball shooting wizard
Build up the defences and air ones too,
Including my wizard tower
Upgrading everything possible,
I can't lose any fights.

Lola Sargeant (10)
Rushmere Hall Primary School, Ipswich

Candyland Fantasy!

I'm in a land made out of candy,
There's a chocolate tower on a hill,
I'm really, really hungry,
I think I'll take a bite.
There's a river made of jelly,
And a coca-cola fountain,
I never want to wake up,
I taste sugar in the air,
There's a forest of strawberry laces,
But over there in the distance,
Something I've never seen,
A giant squishy marshmallow.
I climb up to the top,
I eat from top to bottom,
But when I hit the ground,
I wake up on the floor.
I get back into bed and notice I have no pillow.

Alexander Bark (11)
Rushmere Hall Primary School, Ipswich

A Singer's Dream

Millions of people staring,
At the TV screen.
My family looking onwards,
Clapping and cheering along.
My voice proud and hopeful,
Echoing through the halls.
All the famous places,
Stuck in front of me.
Soon the Sydney Opera House,
Is soon all in my sight
The O2 arena spread in front of me,
All the people riveted to the spot
My private plane flying,
All over the world for me.
When I sing out loud,
My fears all desert me.
This is all a singer's dream.

Bryony Seabrook (11)
Rushmere Hall Primary School, Ipswich

Hamster

A hamster inside a cage,
A cage inside a room,
A room inside a house,
A house within a road,
A road within a country,
A country within the world.

I fear,
I cry,
That my hamster might die.

What if my hamster escapes the cage?
What if it escapes the room?
What if it escapes the house?
What if it escapes the road?
What if it escapes the country?
What if it escapes the world?
I will never see it again...

Fraya Garwood (11)
Rushmere Hall Primary School, Ipswich

Trapped In A Cage

Unwanted and isolated,
I was heartbroken,
A carousel of thoughts whirled in my head,
I felt like an animal trapped in the zoo.

Unwanted and isolated,
I had a fog of thoughts,
My eyes filled with tears,
My stomach was in knots
Lost all trust, forgotten all hope.

Unwanted and isolated,
I was betrayed,
You stepped into my life,
You hurt me,
Stabbed me,
You left me
Unwanted and isolated.

Jessica Harvey (11)
Rushmere Hall Primary School, Ipswich

I Am A Star

I travel the world in the night,
I never see the light of day,
I never feel the warmth of the sun,
I am a star.

I am never seen behind the clouds,
But I am seen in a clear sky,
I am always stuck here,
Only moving when told to.

I want to travel the world in the day,
I want to travel the world as a human would,
I am a star,
But I wake up and realise it is all a dream.

Emily Hawkridge (10)
Rushmere Hall Primary School, Ipswich

Trapped In A Cage With The Truth

The truth is a prison
I was betrayed
You hurt me
You stabbed me in the back
My brain is a carousel
And my thoughts whirl around on top
I'm an animal in a zoo
A way of getting rid of me
Why can't you stay?

The truth is a prison
My eyes filled with tears
My stomach in knots
Lost all trust, forgotten all hope.

Olivia Hall (11)
Rushmere Hall Primary School, Ipswich

Shyness

I am extremely shy
When I don't want to talk I dream of being in the sky.
I fly just to get away.
I am mostly there all day
I am extremely shy.

I am extremely shy
I am an expert on how to fly
I feel as though I'm never going to die.
As I soar I feel weightless
No more craziness
I am extremely shy.

Holly Misselbrook (10)
Rushmere Hall Primary School, Ipswich

The Horizon

The horizon was over the hills,
The horizon was setting,
The horizon was beautiful colours,
The horizon was my world.

The horizon was over the hills,
The horizon was rising,
The horizon was my dream,
The horizon was my world.

The horizon was setting for me
The horizon was rising for me.

Ellen Savage (11)
Rushmere Hall Primary School, Ipswich

Lost

The wind made my hair fly
As I walked beneath the high trees,
Soon I noticed that I was lost in the gloomy forest
When I walked past a tree, a new tree formed.
I needed a shelter,
So I looked for a cave
Once I found a cave I saw two beady eyes,
I heard a roar,
I fell backwards,
Everything went black.

Lilly Grace Matthews (11)
Rushmere Hall Primary School, Ipswich

Dreaming The Dream Of Seeing Your Hero

I dream of seeing a swimmer
Or maybe a footballer
It's definitely a sports person
I wish they'd come out from behind the curtain.

They're definitely from the Olympics
Maybe they could give me some tips
Oh I've got it, they're a runner
There before me is Mo Farah.

Samuel Davey (10)
Rushmere Hall Primary School, Ipswich

Footballer

I am an amazing brilliant footballer,
I see a ball get kicked,
I smell fresh air entering my lungs
I drink some cold strawberry water.
It tasted very nice,
I am an amazing brilliant footballer.
I am a football boot collector
I am an amazing brilliant footballer
With a very good life.

Ashton Symonds (10)
Rushmere Hall Primary School, Ipswich

My Own Head

Though others would dream
Of having a unicorn ride
I decide to turn up the stream
And dream of those stories I read
Which I store inside my own head
In there is an idea that
Maybe those stories give me reasons to dread.
I'm just happy after each one of them
I wake in bed.

Jessica Whiffin (11)
Rushmere Hall Primary School, Ipswich

I Am

I am in a world of amazing and outstanding
superpowers.
I can turn invisible or fly
I can sneak up on people and mess around with them.
I can capture the baddest of criminals.

We can go and steal some pizzas
And money, rob banks
Or if I was flying I would fly into space.

Samuel Radley (10)
Rushmere Hall Primary School, Ipswich

Untitled

I am scared and alone
I cry at the face of danger
I scream when I see a spider
I sob when I am alone
I am lost and alone.

I am happy and courageous
I laugh in the face of danger
I smile at the birds
I sing when I'm alone
I am happy and courageous!

Zander James (11)
Rushmere Hall Primary School, Ipswich

A Dragon Ride

I heard a tap at the window
So I leapt out of bed
I saw a dragon's head
Wow look at that!
I opened my window
A dragon's paw reached to me
I stood and slid down its back
We rode up high
Up high to the clouds
The clouds felt like...
Marshmallows!

Lacey Goodwin (10)
Rushmere Hall Primary School, Ipswich

My Nightmare

I am lost and lonely
I am in a different world
I am being followed by a stranger
I am scared of what will happen next.

I am lost and confused
I am surrounded by ghosts
I am in a ghost town
I am frightened

Am I going to die?

Lucy Rose Smith (11)
Rushmere Hall Primary School, Ipswich

Crazy Mess Of Dreams

D oes everybody scream from a bad dream?
R oosters sing a deadly song
E h! Stop it
A nd I want to kill those roosters
M onster roosters
S hut up!

Kayleigh Rose Garrett (11)
Rushmere Hall Primary School, Ipswich

Magical World

I had a dream last night
But it wasn't a fright
It was quite nice
There were no mice.

Soon I hear
Something is near
Oh look
This is better than reading a book

There's bears scratching
Dragons snoring
Trotting unicorns
I like this, is there any popcorn?

Songs being sung
This is better than being young
More, more, more.
Mermaids splashing on the shore.

Yells of laughter
This is going to have a happily ever after
Rainbows spilling from the sky
I'm really not telling a lie.

Come on, before the day's done
You need to have lots of fun
Wow look at this
Can't think this this.

Is awesome chocolate grass
I wouldn't pass
Sticky toffee walls
Chocolate waterfalls.

Is it over?
Oh, a four-headed clover!
I've got luck
Oh golden muck.

Oh no the clock said seven
Not eleven
There was a sun beam
This was the world of my dream!

Gracie Collison (9)
Sandringham & West Newton CE Primary School, West Newton

The Sounds In My Dreams

Sometimes the sounds in my dreams are the ghosts,
Howling like a hungered wolf,
Sometimes the sounds are the pink unicorns,
Playing with one another.

Sometimes the sounds in my dreams are the worms
Wriggling out of the ground
Sometimes the sounds are the hairy spiders,
Trying to catch their dinner.

Sometimes the sounds in my dreams are the swords
Clashing to win the battle
Sometimes the sounds are the digging miners
Going back to the surface.

Sometimes the sounds in my dreams are the pigs,
Grunting and snorting, 'Hello.'
Sometimes the sounds are the crying babies
Weeping for their mums and dads.

It is a shame that these are in a dream,
And no one else will listen
It is a shame that these are in a dream
And no one else will listen.

Jasper Pike (9)
Sandringham & West Newton CE Primary School, West Newton

Unicorns

U p in the sky where nothing is real when the sounds of unicorns neigh

N othing is evil and nothing is a sound of a seal!

I t never thunders and it is always safe

C louds are always glistening upon moon-like ocean

O h I hear a song that's fading as I walk away.

R oaring lions as loud as full volumed music

N ine unicorns come out every morning and bring the golden yellow sun up

S adly there are no normal animals up here so we bring them up from earth...

I wish this wasn't a dream.

Nina Daisy Fowler (9)
Sandringham & West Newton CE Primary School, West Newton

Untitled

The sounds of your worst nightmare
What can I hear?
I hear somebody shed a tear
I can hear the spiders spin and spin.
I hear a tin rolling by the door.

The windows smash and break
A car has crashed... *Bang!*
Then a loud yelp
A whole team helps.
But then the death of them all.

Then the loud moaning
Then the running down the hall
That really is quite tall
All the dead bodies,
Rapidly I wake up to find,
I'm safe at home on the floor!

Tyler Kerry (9)
Sandringham & West Newton CE Primary School, West Newton

Wonderful World

The bright stars are like suns
Like magical suns.
The moon is like a big star,
That always comes out at night
I hear the calls
Of the magical stars.
When it's sunlight,
You can see the magic of birds talking
The water is nice, it helps plants grow
The houses are chocolate
The grass is mint
The water is filled with orange juice.
The trees are made of balloons
The sky is rainbow-coloured
I can hear the water plunging
The wind blowing hardly
The grass crunching.

Jack James Miller (9)
Sandringham & West Newton CE Primary School, West Newton

Sounds On The Pitch

Sounds of the football boots,
Coming out of the tunnel,
Everybody clapping,
Saying, 'Go on, go on!'

The first whistle goes
Referee gives a free kick,
Fifty yards out.
Saying, 'Great tackle!'

Manager shouting on the sideline,
Before the very last minute
The final whistle finally goes.

I cannot wait until my next game
This job will truly be the best
I cannot wait till I am older.
It truly will be the best.

Henry Benjamin James (9)
Sandringham & West Newton CE Primary School, West Newton

Getting Lost In The Woods At Night!

The sounds when I scatter,
Go all through the woods,
All I hear are gunshots,
Clashing against pots,
Trees wafting side to side,
While branches collide,
Vampires chasing me,
What shall I do?
Lakes roughly splash,
I need a weapon, but I have no cash!
I hear wolves howling,
One is prowling,
I think there's a blue moon,
Or could it be a cocoon?
I'm just a baby,
I'm frightened!
Suddenly I awoke,
Phew, it was just a dream.

Maddy Taylor (9)
Sandringham & West Newton CE Primary School, West Newton

Horrid Noises

Spiders tinkling in your kitchen
Giants coming to your bedroom,
Sharks flipping in your swimming pool,
Suddenly giant bullies charging at you.

Frightening snakes wrapped around you,
The snakes laughing while they're being tickled,
Lions licking their lips at you,
Thinking they're going to eat you.

Brothers and sisters screaming,
At massive snakes hissing
Then the animal keeper came to take them,
That's how my dream ended!

Lilly Clare Hickling (8)
Sandringham & West Newton CE Primary School, West Newton

Monster Madness

I had a dream last night,
It gave me a fright,
There were hideous monsters in my house,
But they were as quiet as a mouse.

As they tiptoed through the house,
I swore I could hear a giant woodlouse,
Crawling at the end of my wooden bed,
(Even though there are lots in the old, creaky
garden shed.)

Suddenly, I woke up,
Realising it was just a dream,
I was in my mum and dad's bed,
And they were cuddling close to me.

Clara Elizabeth Moreland (8)
Sandringham & West Newton CE Primary School, West Newton

Scary Noises

First I hear horses,
Then I hear a fright
Soon I hear something else,
I don't want to find.

Now I should go
It's coming closer
I go into the night
Then I start to hear footsteps.

Soon I get closer
Then I get close
Now I'm touching it
I think I should go!

Then I get scared,
I run and I run
Then I wake up and say
'Phew, it was just a dream.'

Jasmina Gadiwala (9)
Sandringham & West Newton CE Primary School, West Newton

The Sounds Of The Police Girl

The sounds of a police girl,
Might be just near your ear,
The sirens when a police girl goes past,
Are really not near.

As I'm back to sleep,
Just by my ear,
The shooting of guns,
I should never go near.

Till the next sound comes,
She's walking past,
With the radio,
I find my pillow and back to sleep I go
When I grow up I can't wait to be this.

Sienna May (8)
Sandringham & West Newton CE Primary School, West Newton

The Sounds Of My Dream

N othing moved in that peculiar minute,

I t all happened very quickly,

G hastly monsters growling at me

H ardly any precious space,

T ime was sadly running out

M ake lovely time, oh please Lord

A n amazing fierce and scary monster

R an at me and caught me, noo!

E verywhere I sleep, I dream this terrible dream.

Thomas Strudwick (8)

Sandringham & West Newton CE Primary School, West Newton

Sweet Racing In Candy Land

It's midnight in my dream
I hear people racing,
Engines starting
The clapping of hands.

Then I hear a loud bang!
Followed by chomping,
It gets louder and louder,
I can't figure out what it is,

Voices shouting, 'You can do it!'
More chomping, crunching and gulping,
'What could this be?'
I wonder...

Chloe Southwell (8)
Sandringham & West Newton CE Primary School, West Newton

Bells And Laughs

Hearing church bells,
As I start to sit in the crumbly seat.
Bang! goes the doors,
It gives me a massive fright,
It's those creepy clowns again
As I stand up,
I shout, 'Run!'
As the clowns start to laugh
We all start to run!
As I wake up
I shout, 'Mum!'

Ella Southwell (8)
Sandringham & West Newton CE Primary School, West Newton

An Architect

A lthough it's not a simple job, it's my dream
R epeatedly you build things
C ars and motorcycles always built
H igh and low quiet buildings alike
I nventions galore
T echnical at most
E xciting
C reative
T remendous above all.

Giovanni Giubileo (8)
Sandringham & West Newton CE Primary School, West Newton

Sea Away

S eeing what is left from the sandy shore
E els going bizarre and much more,
A click of my fingers

A nd everything lingers
W hat can we do?
A hh look it is something misty blue
Y es! It was just a dream.

Taylor Ashton Winsor (9)
Sandringham & West Newton CE Primary School, West Newton

Dream Train

D riving on the choo choo train
R oaring of the noisy engine
E lectricity, bangs flash all over
A larms from the booming bright fire bell
M unching of the children eating sandwiches, yum!
S houting of the scared children.

Stanley Thomas Farr-James (8)
Sandringham & West Newton CE Primary School, West Newton

Doctors

D reaming to be a doctor and saving people

R escuing people and saving them

E verybody is snoring quietly

A larms go off loudly

M any people are screaming at night

S ounds are coming from outside.

Kateryna Musgrave (8)

Sandringham & West Newton CE Primary School, West Newton

The Clown

Clown o'clown
Why are you down?

Clown o'clown
Why are you so mean?

Clown o'clown
Why aren't you happy?

Clown o'clown
The circus is in town.

Clown o'clown
So shake off your frown.

Clown o'clown
Have some fun, fun, fun!

Franciszek Teliczan (10)
St Felix RC Primary School, Haverhill

The Never-Ending Dream

My thoughts feel heavy, as I lift off the ground
I don't know what to expect
My imagination is running wild
as I go round and round.

I open my eyes to a mystical land
Full of crazy creatures and hypnotising happiness
It's a lovely place or is it not?
I see the queen with her Sceptre that must have cost
a grand.

A golden dress whips past me
The thick brunette fur tangles around Belle
The thought of leaving distracts my mind.
Next thing I know the beast has invited me for tea.

Once we have moved swiftly on
The wrappers crinkle under my feet
As the chocolate melts through my hands
and we have finished our never-ending dream.

Well at least for tonight...

Eluned Morgan-Owen (9) & Grace
St Felix RC Primary School, Haverhill

My Head Fell Off!

I went out
The other day
My head fell off
And rolled away
But when I noticed
It was gone
I picked it up
And put it on
I went out
The following day
My leg fell off
And jumped away
So I hopped to find it
And found it and put it on
I hope that does not fall off again.

Kathy Ann Wirowski (10)
St Felix RC Primary School, Haverhill

Nightmares To Dreams

Nightmare runs through the night
You really don't want to bump into her
Really the black horse will give you such a fright
She's no night kitty, she will not purr
Or give you a candy cane.
She only runs through the night
Her midnight mane
Carries no light
And it is not fun
Take her mane
Turn it into something good.
Maybe the little bit vain
Miss Red Riding Hood
Or maybe you dream lame
Or maybe you're a professional footballer
Or even an amazing poet
Stretch that dream taller
And achieve then you'll know it
When you've lassoed Nightmare
Because you'll be there...
In your fantasy dream come true.

Jasmine Nungari Marshall (10)
St Felix RC Primary School, Haverhill

Mr Unicorn

Mr Unicorn, where are you?
Mr Unicorn, what shall I do?
Your rainbow tail sparkles in the light
How about we fly a kite?
Your golden horn is so shiny
I can see your tiny light
Throughout the night
You love to jump on the clouds
You never gave me a frown
Bye-bye for now
I will see you tonight
In my wildest dream.

Nakita Van Aswegen (10)
St Felix RC Primary School, Haverhill

Once Upon A Dream

Once upon a dream
I was in a stream.
Once upon a dream
The stream was made of ice cream!
Once upon a dream
The ice cream was in a flower -
Not at all like a shower,
Just ice cream in a flower!
Not at all like a tower!
Once upon a dream
I looked down in the air.
Once upon a dream,
I saw a pear!
Once upon a dream
The pear was hiding under a chair -
Not at all willing to share!
Once upon a dream
I dived into the sea.
Once upon a dream,
A man rubbed his hands in glee.
Once upon a dream
I'm back in bed
Once upon a dream...

Claudia Bergin (9)
St Felix RC Primary School, Haverhill

Pokémon Go/Pikachu

Once upon a dream
I was at home then my dad came,
He gave me a packet of Pokémon cards,
I opened it and got Pikachu ex,
My mum and dad sent me to bed,
I brushed my teeth and got into bed,
I drifted off to sleep into a world of dreams
I spawned into the world of Pokémon,
Pikachu was standing next to me,
I threw a Pokéball at him,
Hip hip hooray, I caught Pikachu,
Then I saw Team Rocket verses Team Instinct
and Pikachu,
I spawned back home and said,
'It was just a dream after all!'

Cody Armstrong (9)
St Felix RC Primary School, Haverhill

Team Rocket Blasts Off Again

There was a Pokémon trainer called Ash
And his Pokémon partner was called Pikachu.
His partner was an electric type.
Then there were bad guys,
They were spying on Ash and Pikachu.
Their mission was to steal Pikachu.
Their name was Team Rocket,
They got a hand grappling gun.
They aimed at Pikachu and they fired.
It grappled onto Pikachu
And it pulled Pikachu towards them.
Then Ash said to Pikachu, 'Use a thunderbolt,' and shocked them.
Then Team Rocket blasted off to a secret forest.

Tyler Cardoso (9)
St Felix RC Primary School, Haverhill

The Eagle Of The Mountain

It was once said the eagle of the mountain
Soared high in the sky
Up, up as high as he could fly.

He lived on the mountain at the peak
He guarded it with his beak
Nobody knew what he spoke
For he spoke in riddles.

So go away from the crimson killer, for his riddles kill
He comes in disguise behind dark glasses
If you'd get too close he'd kill no matter what class.

The dim light became more clear
Nobody was there
For the eagle had done his job...

Oscar Clay (9)
St Felix RC Primary School, Haverhill

The Secret Mystery

Once upon a magical time
Listen close to this pantomime
Fairies and creatures hide in the woods
It seems so fun everyone should!

But then evil strikes
And everyone shouts, 'Yikes!'
Can it get worse?
Yes! Thunder strike on my bike!

But who will save the day?
It's only the 16th of May
Nor you or me know
I hope the pirates don't show!

Now we are totally safe.
Do you like my story?
And do you have faith?

Anna-Grace Mathew (10)
St Felix RC Primary School, Haverhill

The Flying Bus

Once their was a boy
Jeffy was his name
He lived with his mum and dad
In a mansion made of candy
Balcony made of candy canes,
The structure made of gummy,
He had a pet unicorn and Pikachu
So he basically had everything.
Had sweets for dinner,
Drinks and slushies.
His mum's car was a cloud,
His school was a castle,
His teacher was a dragon,
He had a very weird school trip.
He went to the moon on a flying bus.
And that was the end.

Ryan Hammond (9)
St Felix RC Primary School, Haverhill

This Strange Place

The planets came by,
Then I said, 'Hi!'
They looked at me and wondered why,
The sky turned black to pink to yellow,
Then I saw a strange fellow,
He had two eyes,
and wore some ties,
he pulled me by,
We flew like birds,
But he didn't talk,
There was a meteor,
But we couldn't walk,
It then turned red,
and I was in bed,
I remembered the view and went back to sleep
That was it,
I was happy now, tonight I will be safe now.

Juvi Danielle Sason Carandang (9)
St Felix RC Primary School, Haverhill

C.I.R.C.U.S

I enter my dream - it's red and white,
Can you guess? Yes! I'm eating pink, fluffy candyfloss,
As some of the crowd look scruffy,
It's time to begin my favourite part

The big top lights are glowing,
And the ringmaster is singing,
As the trapeze is flinging.

It's knife throwing, acrobats,
Wow! It's amazing, my pink, fluffy candyfloss is gone,
Now it's time to wake,
The sunlight replaces the lights that shone.

Hollie Buckingham (10)
St Felix RC Primary School, Haverhill

Nightmare!

N othing to save you in a forest dark at night

I mages of wolves, spiders and all creatures bad

G ory blood all around dripping from trees

H ow it is scary, you don't know what's lurking around

T oo scary for me!

M any creatures lurk around

A nything to save me? I don't know

R are for me to survive

E veryone in bed, having a dream except for me with
a... nightmare!

Sofia Emily Rinaldi (9)
St Felix RC Primary School, Haverhill

Sleeping In Maths Class

Oh is this a dream?
All I see is a chocolate stream
Unicorns, fairies everywhere,
All I can do is stop and stare
Suddenly, I feel like someone is watching me
As I am drained of all my glee.
Clowns, monsters in the air,
They're all walking everywhere,
One... two... three... four...
Pop! I'm there no more
I'm in a maths class,
I woke up in a blast
Oh it was just a dream.

Lucy Murrell (10)
St Felix RC Primary School, Haverhill

Unicorn Paradise

I look down, I see rainbow-coloured cotton candy,
Suddenly a unicorn kneels by my feet as if I am
a queen.
I call the unicorn Miss Unicorn!
She neighs in mid-air so I hold her horn
We go to the ground and what do I see?
My new fantastic castle
The rooftops are whippy cream,
The door is muddy, hard toffee!
The walls are made of pinky cupcake holders.
I look down, I see rainbow-coloured cotton candy.

Zoe Olivia Boreham (9)
St Felix RC Primary School, Haverhill

All Over The World

All over the world,
The world awaits,
With my mates,
From gazing up at the stars
To driving fast cars.
I've got the chance in France.

When you go to Spain
You don't want it to rain.
Flowing through Mexico,
To eating tacos on Tuesday.
Different types of transport,
Plane, cruise, train,
Zoom, zoom, zoom!

All over the world.

Joshua King (9)
St Felix RC Primary School, Haverhill

The U Dream!

I dream inside my bed
Dreams floating around my head,
Blue, yellow, purple and pink,
Get ready because this is a link.

The link to my favourite dream,
Inside there is a horsey kind of team
Some of them are big, large or newborn,
And on top of their heads there is a swirly whirly horn!

Do you know what kind of horse I am thinking of?
It is a unicorn!

Marta Grzegorczyk (9)
St Felix RC Primary School, Haverhill

Following A Butterfly

As I sit on grass as green as can be,
A butterfly hovers over me.
Like an angel graceful as she flies,
I gaze at her natural beauty.
I get up and follow her.
Who knows what adventures she'll take me on.
I'll just wait and see as she takes me to an
imaginary land.
She flies away and I wake up to greet the day!

Where will your imagination take you?

Evie Grace Naylor (8)
St Felix RC Primary School, Haverhill

Sweetie Land

In Sweetie Land
Far away
I can see a Milky Way
Candyfloss as some trees
I can see sugar leaves
Floating down from the trees
Sweetie people come to me
With sugar lumps and lots of tea
Choco pops are so sweet
Houses made from toffee and treats,
Tiny lollies just to eat
And fizzy pops
Yum... yum... yum
All in
Sweetie Land.

Cahir Catherine Williams (9)
St Felix RC Primary School, Haverhill

Once Upon A Dream (A Menace)

The Menace uses spiders as a prank
Dennis the Menace and his lads!
Minnie the Minx using mice to make the cats bite
Gnasher and Gnipper having a pie too.
Pie Face having a party with his friends.
Cannonballing walker is what we do
Boom, boom, boom,
Help, help, help,
I am telling my father!
Dennis the Menace and his lads!

Catherine Anne Theresa Goring (9)
St Felix RC Primary School, Haverhill

My Future Dream!

I dream about the future,
I wonder where I'll go,
I'll become a pilot and fly to Mexico.
Next I go to England
Then I go to Norway
And fly to Australia
After that it's off to Brazil
I dream about the future
I wonder where I go...
But then I realise it was
Just a dream
But I'm becoming a pilot.

Luca Lambert (9)
St Felix RC Primary School, Haverhill

Unicorn

Beautiful unicorn
You have a beautiful horn
You have candy cane-pink hair
And I just stare.

You are pretty
Like a baby kitty
Sweet fast rides
Then I hide.

And when I laugh
Your magical multicoloured tail swings
And at night your hair is glowing string
And every night you get a new ring.

Weronika Lubinska (9)
St Felix RC Primary School, Haverhill

Famous

F ans waving and cheering, calling your name

A step anywhere and people will recognise you

M ocking your enemies when they face you

O h how lucky you are to be famous!

U ttering the best words about you

S o if you like having fans and money then being famous is the right thing for you.

Felix Jose (9)

St Felix RC Primary School, Haverhill

Dreams And Nightmares

There are two dimensions
Dreams and nightmares
Dreams are happy
And nightmares are creepy
Dreams have unicorns, fish and rainbows
Nightmares have death, clowns and empty places
I prefer dreams because I like to take a look around.
But nightmares have been stuck
In one empty, fatal room...

Michal Wargin (10)
St Felix RC Primary School, Haverhill

The Sea And Stars

Glittering, shimmering, shining in the sea,
Where I stay there I feel shocked
Where I see the darkness.
I see the bright beautiful stars up in the sky
Everyone is asleep.
But I stand on the dashing water touching the warm water from the sea.
And I float like a spirit when he goes to heaven.

Maya Glowacki (9)
St Felix RC Primary School, Haverhill

Fantasy All Night

Dragons with fire breath
Unicorns with rainbow glitter manes.
Monsters green and red
Ready to give you a scare.
All dancing in the moonlit sky...

Alexandra Graham (8)
St Felix RC Primary School, Haverhill

The Secret Dream World

I see a fairy bed as fluffy as a feather
I see a unicorn as beautiful as a butterfly
I see a fairy house as small as a dice
I see a fairy garden as pretty as a rose bush.
I am with a butterfly fluttering above
I am with a cat as fluffy as a fluffball
I am with a bird who has lost a feather
I am with a parrot who loves to play and dance,
I am in a fairy house as pretty as a cat
I am in a butterfly's mouth as slimy as some tree sap.
I am in a beehive as small as a mouse.
I feel happy like never before
I feel wonderful
I feel joyful.
I turn into a pony as tall as a table
I turn into a hedgehog as spiky as a thorn
I turn into a cart as pretty as some glitter.
I am waking up, it's like a dream come true.

Emily Rose Morton (8)
Swanton Abbott Community Primary School, Swanton Abbott

The Mythical Creatures

There were visitors at the stables
Unicorns in the stalls
Name labels hang around their necks
While ponies play with balls!

Pegasus fly around the place,
Refusing to come down
Their beautiful long faces
Float gently all around.

It's exciting, all the mythical creatures
So we all go off and explore,
Forgetting about the horses and ponies
Not noticing my pony was no more.

My pony Shadow - he's gone I realise!
I climb onto a unicorn's back
We fly all over the woods
To see a pony munching on a haystack!

Once we're home again,
I'm really happy
Shadow's home safe,
He's never going ever
Again!

Ellie Simmons (9)
Swanton Abbott Community Primary School, Swanton Abbott

The Magic Of The Woods

What's that?
A twig or branch snapped,
My heart is beating fast
There's magic in my breath,
I can feel something controlling me,
Then suddenly puff, boom,
There is silence all round.

I can see something out there,
But I can't see what it was,
Maybe a black cat,
Or the deep magic of the woods,
Whatever it is, it's coming towards,
Out of the mist came an emerald-green dragon,
Wings stretched out, eyes wide,
It strides towards me...

It looks at me
And where I stand,
This is my friend, my new friend,
I hope I see him again
Into my imagination he has come,
And now in my bed I will dream of him,
All alone...

Millie Isabel Karim (9)
Swanton Abbott Community Primary School, Swanton Abbott

Gazing Through My Window

Gazing through my window,
I'm mesmerised by the sky.
Gazing through my window,
I feel like saying goodbye.
Gazing through my window,
I see swords and guns.
Gazing through my window,
why couldn't it be nice blueberry buns?
Gazing through my window,
soldiers and bombs.
Gazing through my window,
it's like church bells doing a thousand bongs.
Gazing through my window,
terrified and amazed.
Gazing through my window,
gazing and gazing I've gazed and gazed.
Gazing through my window,
I'll call the evil lords with a bang, bang, bang.
I get pulled through my window,
pulled into reality and realise it was a dream.

Isabella McKnespiey (9)
Swanton Abbott Community Primary School, Swanton Abbott

The Black Cat

A black cat stops in my path
An angry storm looms above,
The trees whisper, 'Turn back now!'
I know it's too late,
A gold wisp twirls around me
A clap of thunder lights the trees,
Fire is blown along in the breeze,
I hear a song, low and evil,
The cat now has a jar,
In the jar there is a glowing pink mist,
The jar breaks! I hope it's okay
How do I get out of this dream?
Black magic fills the air.
I feel scared.
Everything is turning, twisting, turning.
The fire is a bird.
Suddenly, I fall.
I am cold as ice.
Don't disturb the black cat,
Or your life will be cursed!

Rebecca Mae Strawson (8)
Swanton Abbott Community Primary School, Swanton Abbott

No Family

I can see
The big tall vase trees,
Nature crawling around me
Bark laying on the ground silent.

I can see
Twigs hanging on the trees bare
Leaves moving gently
Bees buzzing.

I can feel
I can feel nerves in the rainforest
Scared
Frightened
Nerves
All the emotions at once.

Ouch - there was no family
Grrr! A fox growled
I was standing there
No people - no animals.

Louise Hurrell (9)
Swanton Abbott Community Primary School, Swanton Abbott

Dreamy Cat

There was a cat called Elizabeth the first
and she fell asleep.

And she dreamed that she had a nine-year-old
Elizabeth the first was so happy.

Whenever she was there
she ran away and gets lost in the woods.

When she was in the woods,
she was sad but she found her way home

Then she woke up
from her dream and she was not happy because it was
not real...

Cia Smith (9)
Swanton Abbott Community Primary School, Swanton Abbott

The Baby Unicorn

The black forest glows,
As night becomes day,
Unicorns arrive,
As calmness and happiness flow through my body.
Whilst the enigmatic foals
Grow their horns,
And sparks fly overhead
As a sign of first magic
'Please don't wake me up,'
Then... it happens, I am woken
I see daylight,
I open my window,
And I swear I see a unicorn
Before my eyes, I see a swirl of magic dust!

Halle Mynett-Smith (8)
Swanton Abbott Community Primary School, Swanton Abbott

Walking Upon A...

In the distance something's stumbling awkwardly
As if it was trying to escape
With Freddie, Corey, Will, Max B, Max G and Tyler.
All my close friends.
Walking upon a moonlit planet
As alabaster as can be
Many galaxies away.
I swear I see clown feet on an athlete's body
And Lionel Messi's head all dripping with lava.
'Please tell me this is a dream...'

Oliver Bunton-Butler (8)
Swanton Abbott Community Primary School, Swanton Abbott

My Unicorn

My unicorn flies in the mystic air
Does magic with her horn
She's my best friend
She plays dance and does magic with me,
Helps me with my tests.
She loves me and I love her.
Her magic helps me with my life.
One day she flies away from me and I never see
her again.
Her swishy tail and her magical horn, gone!
Our friendship breaks for once and for all.

Mia Lofty (8)
Swanton Abbott Community Primary School, Swanton Abbott

Unicorns

I was in a dream world with my dog, Rusty.
Just then I heard a rustle in the leaves and a clown
jumped up.
It took Rusty,
So I went to look for him
Instead I found a unicorn
It said that it would help me find my puppy.
So we set off.
The white unicorn's back
I sunk into her soft fur,
Then we found my puppy
All curled up in a bush.

Lyra Hall (8)
Swanton Abbott Community Primary School, Swanton Abbott

Stormy Night

One stormy night I had a dream.
I woke up and I saw a dusky moon.
It was shimmering in the moonlight
That day I was walking through the forest.
The birds were singing and there was wildlife
around me.
Rabbits were hopping around
And baby deer were learning how to walk
Lots of roses surrounded me with lots of other flowers.

Ellie Summer Oakley (9)
Swanton Abbott Community Primary School, Swanton Abbott

The Woods

The rushing leaves brush me,
Was that you maybe?
Who are you?
Give me a clue.

The brambles prick me,
What is that ahead of me?
Animals' swords maybe.

A phoenix of power and glory,
Will I come out alive, Dory?
My friend...

Freddie Wilson (8)
Swanton Abbott Community Primary School, Swanton Abbott

Riding Dragon

In the grass
I can see a riding dragon
Lurking for some food
Fish or maybe rabbit
Mice or maybe mole
Riding dragon, riding dragon
On I get
Up we go up into the sky
Riding dragon, riding dragon.

Thomas Aldous (7)
Swanton Abbott Community Primary School, Swanton Abbott

Lizard Land

I can see giant green and black scaly lizards
In a house and one is after me
As I run, I know it's no use
It has caught me
I am confused and scared at the same time.

Max Brackpool (8)
Swanton Abbott Community Primary School, Swanton Abbott

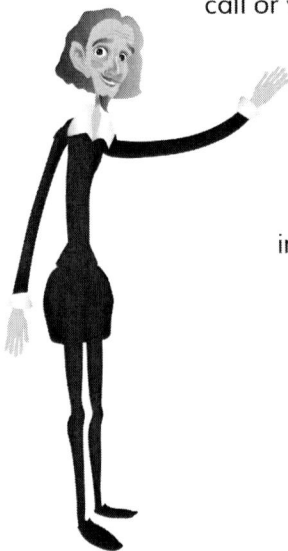